In The Wild

Jaguars

Stephanie St. Pierre

Heinemann Library
Chicago, Illinois

Customer Service 888-454-2279

Visit our website at www.heinemannlibrary.com

Designed by Depke Design
Printed in Hong Kong

05 04 03
10 9 8 7 6 5 4 3 2

Library of Congress Cataloging-in-Publication Data
St. Pierre, Stephanie.
    Jaguars / by Stephanie St. Pierre.
        p. cm. -- (In the wild)
Includes bibliographical references (p.   ).
    ISBN 1-58810-108-8 (lib. bdg.)   ISBN 1-58810-381-1 (pbk. bdg.)
    1. Jaguar--Juvenile literature. [1. Jaguar.] I. Title. II. Series.
    QL737.C23 S713 2001
    599.75'5--dc21
                                        00-012652

Acknowledgments
The author and publishers are grateful to the following for permission to reproduce copyright material:
Mary Ann McDonald/Corbis, p. 4 (far left); Tom Brakefield/Corbis, pp. 4 (center), 5, 15; Darrell Gulin/Corbis, p. 4 (far right); Michael & Patricia Fogden/Corbis, pp. 6, 7; Tom Brakefield/Bruce Coleman, pp. 8, 11, 13, 16; Tom Brakefield/PictureQuest, p. 9; W. Perry Conway/Corbis, p. 10; Wendy Shattil/Index Stock Imagery/PictureQuest, p. 12; Steve Kaufman/Corbis, p. 14; Kennan Ward/Corbis, p. 17; Francisco Erize/Bruce Coleman, pp. 18, 20; John S. Flannery/Bruce Coleman, p. 19; Erwin & Peggy Bauer/Bruce Coleman, p. 21; Norman Owen Tomalin/Bruce Coleman, p. 22; Kevin Schafer/Corbis, p. 23.

Cover photograph: Micheal & Patricia Fogden/Corbis

Some words are shown in bold, **like this.** You can find out what they mean by looking in the glossary.

Contents

Jaguar Relatives

Jaguars are one of the many kinds of **felines.** Jaguars have brown or yellow fur with dark round markings. Sometimes jaguars are completely black. Jaguars are often confused with their relatives, leopards.

leopard

lion

tiger

Jaguars have bigger heads and thicker bodies than leopards. Their markings are also different. Jaguars are close relatives of tigers and lions.

Where Jaguars Live

Jaguars live in South America and Central America. They live in rain forests, **woodlands,** and **grasslands.** Jaguars do not usually live in the mountains. They often live near water.

Jaguars that live in heavy forest are often much smaller than jaguars that live in grasslands. This is because there is larger **prey** in the grasslands.

The Family

Like most cats, jaguars like to be alone. Young jaguars live with their mothers for two years. Each jaguar has a **home range** and marks where it begins and ends by making scratches in trees and dirt.

Grown males and females may share parts
of their home range. They hunt alone, but
sometimes they roam the forest together.

Swimming

Jaguars like to be near water. They are good swimmers. Jaguars can easily swim across small lakes and rivers. They are also good at fishing.

This jaguar is patiently waiting for a fish.
Sometimes the jaguar swishes the tip of its
tail in the water to lure a fish towards it.

Hunting

Like all cats, jaguars hunt by **stalking prey.**
They get as close as they can to their prey before
leaping on it. They make a quick **kill**
by biting it on the neck.

A large kill may be buried or hidden. The jaguar can come back to eat from it for two or three days.

Climbing

Jaguars are very good tree climbers. They climb trees to rest or to hunt or even to play. This jaguar is having a nap.

Some jaguars hunt monkeys or birds by climbing high into the trees. They can leap quickly from branch to branch chasing their **prey.**

Eating

The jaguar eats all kinds of meat. It will eat cattle, deer, monkeys, birds, fish, lizards, and even alligators and insects. What it eats depends on where it lives.

The jaguar has very strong jaws. This helps
it to kill and eat things with hard shells like
turtles or armadillos. Jaguars will also eat
meat left uneaten by other animals.

Babies

Mother jaguars give birth in a **den.** Thorn **thickets** or under the roots of big trees are good places for a den. There are one to four babies in a **litter.**

Cubs come out of the den to play after about two weeks. Their fur has bigger spots than adult jaguars' fur.

Growing Up

When they are six months old young jaguars start hunting with their mother. They will not hunt alone until they are about two years old.

Young jaguars like to explore. They play at hunting. When they begin hunting by themselves it is time for them to find a new home.

Jaguar Facts

- Jaguars can roar. They are often heard roaring in the forest at night.

- Jaguars are almost never seen during the day.

- Jaguars almost never attack people, but they will follow them along forest paths.

- The black marking on the jaguar's fur is called a rosette. It is a circle with a spot in the middle.

Glossary

den safe, hidden living space

feline family of animals that includes all kinds of cats

grassland area of land with few trees but lots of tall grass

litter group of babies born together

lure bait to trick a fish

home range area of land a cat lives on

kill dead animal to be eaten

prey animals hunted for food

rain forest area of land covered by tall trees and many thick layers of plants

stalk watching and carefully following

thicket area of tangled branches

woodland area of land covered by trees with some open spaces

Index

More Books to Read

Cowcher, Helen. *Jaguar*. New York: Scholastic, Inc., 1997.

Welsbacher, Anne. *Jaguars*. Minneapolis, Minn.: Abdo Publishing Co., 2000.